The Future of TECHNOLOGY

What Is the Future of Drones?

Stuart A. Kallen

ReferencePoint Press®

San Diego, CA

© 2017 ReferencePoint Press, Inc.
Printed in the United States

For more information, contact:
ReferencePoint Press, Inc.
PO Box 27779
San Diego, CA 92198
www.ReferencePointPress.com

LIBRARY OF CONGRESS CATALOGING-IN-PUBLICATION DATA

Names: Kallen, Stuart A., 1955- author.
Title: What is the future of drones? / by Stuart A. Kallen.
Description: San Diego, CA : ReferencePoint Press, Inc., [2016] | Series: The future of technology | Audience: Grades 9-12.
Identifiers: LCCN 2016018734 (print) | LCCN 2016020411 (ebook) | ISBN 9781682820629 (hardback) | ISBN 9781682820636 (eBook)
Subjects: LCSH: Drone aircraft--Juvenile literature. | Aeronautics, Commercial--Juvenile literature.
Classification: LCC UG1242.D7 K35 2016 (print) | LCC UG1242.D7 (ebook) | DDC 629.133--dc23
LC record available at https://lccn.loc.gov/2016018734

Contents

Important Events in the Development of Drones

1944
During World War II the US Navy develops the PB4Y-1 unmanned aerial vehicle (UAV), flown by remote control to deliver explosives to German targets.

1958
Congress creates the Federal Aviation Administration (FAA) to regulate and oversee all aspects of American civil aviation.

1978
The Israelis deploy the Scout, a small fiberglass drone that can transmit real-time, 360-degree surveillance data via a television camera in its central turret.

2000
The CIA begins flying unarmed surveillance drones over Afghanistan.

1940 1950 ••• 1970 1980 ••• 2000

1951
The US Air Force deploys the first jet-propelled drone, the Ryan Firebee, which is used as an aerial target for gunnery practice and air-to-air combat training.

1986
The US military begins using the Pioneer UAV, a fixed-wing drone developed for reconnaissance, surveillance, target acquisition, and battle damage assessment missions.

1973
In the Yom Kippur War between Israel and Egypt, the Israeli Air Force deploys a fleet of Firebees as decoys, causing the Egyptians to fire their entire supply of missiles at the unmanned planes.

2003
US Customs and Border Protection initiates a drone program to provide intelligence on undocumented immigrants and drug smugglers along the border.

2004
The CIA kills Nek Muhammad Wazir, an insurgent leader in Pakistan, and several other individuals with a drone.

2016
The world's first drone race is held in Dubai, United Arab Emirates.

2011
In North Dakota a US Customs and Border Protection drone is used to assist local police in an armed standoff for the first time.

2013
Online retailer Amazon announces Prime Air, a program to use drones for package delivery in the United States and elsewhere.

2010
In July the website WikiLeaks publishes more than ninety-one thousand classified US military reports that reveal to the public for the first time the top secret use of drones against human targets in Afghanistan, Iran, and elsewhere.

2005　　　　**2010**　　　　**2015**

2009
Two days after his inauguration as US president, Barack Obama authorizes the first drone strike of his administration.

2012
Congress passes the FAA Modernization and Reform Act, which instructs the FAA to integrate drones into US airspace.

2015
The New York City Drone Film Festival is launched to bring attention to cutting edge movies shot with small cameras mounted on drones.

2014
In September the FAA permits the commercial use of drones for the first time, allowing six aerial photo and video production companies to use drones for filming on closed sets.

Introduction

Incredibly Versatile Machines

From Theory to Application

Drones are formally known as unmanned aerial vehicles, or UAVs. They are aircraft remotely controlled by pilots on the ground. Drones were first developed by the military in the 1940s for use in situations where manned flight was considered too risky or difficult. Today the military uses drones for surveillance and combat missions. Military drones can hover over an area for up to seventeen hours at a time and provide commanders with real-time "eye-in-the-sky" imagery of enemy activities on the ground. Drones flown in Afghanistan, Pakistan, and elsewhere are equipped with Hellfire missiles, which can strike targets at a range of about 5 miles (8 km). Consumer drones are much smaller than military drones—about the size of a backpack. But consumer drones carry the same tools used by the military for surveillance and guidance. These tools include video cameras, lasers, Global Positioning System (GPS), radar, and infrared imaging to detect activity in low-light conditions.

In 2014 the *New York Times* published a review of the best-selling DJI Phantom 2 Vision consumer drone. Reviewer Kit Eaton wrote that only five years earlier, such a drone "would have seemed like a science-fiction film prop or a piece of surveillance hardware flown only by the sexiest of superspies."[1] Eaton marveled at the Phantom's ability to shoot videos and photos from more than 1,000 feet (305 m) in the air while relying on a GPS to fly automatically back to its launching point and land on its own. Eaton said the $1,200 drone was "a bit of tomorrow's tech in your hands today."[2]

Today Eaton's comments about "tomorrow's tech" seem almost quaint. An estimated 1 million drones were purchased by US consumers in 2015, and another million were sold in Europe, China, and elsewhere as drones were already starting to make their impact felt in agriculture, energy, security, and entertainment. In 2015 technology futurist Gray Scott commented on the outlook for drones: "We are right on the tip of the iceberg. Within the next five years I believe we're going to see a saturation of drones in the United States; they're going to be extremely common."[3]

The exploding popularity of drones can be traced to the fact that they are incredibly versatile machines. Military planners depend on drones for surveillance and launching missiles at enemies. Consumers and industry have devised altogether different uses for drones. Drones can shoot photos and videos while flying high in the sky or inches off the ground. They can be used to deliver packages and pizzas. Drone cameras provide filmmakers with unique panoramic shots, utility companies with the means to remotely inspect power lines and pipelines, and reporters with a way to capture eye-opening footage of the destruction in war zones.

High-Flying High-Tech

The development of drones parallels advancements in smartphone technology. The miniature cameras, GPS, and advanced data-processing chips developed for cell phones were easily transferred to drones. So while most drones look like little more than a plastic frame and a few rotors, they pack an amazing amount of technology into a small device. This technology allows even amateur pilots to safely launch, land, and navigate drones—most of the time.

Handheld controllers communicate with drones using Wi-Fi, technically known as 2.4 gigahertz radio waves. The GPS relays the craft's location to the controller while keeping a log of the drone's takeoff spot so it can return unassisted. GPS also helps a

A small drone, equipped with a camera, flies above Antarctica. Unmanned aerial vehicles, commonly referred to as drones, are probably best known as weapons of war, but other uses for drones are rapidly gaining attention.

drone hover and correct course when strong winds blow; some drones can remain in place when exposed to wind gusts of 50 miles per hour (80 kph).

In 2016 researchers were striving to integrate artificial intelligence (AI) capabilities into drones. This would make even the simplest hobby drone autonomous; the machine would fly, navigate, hover, and land smoothly without input from a pilot. AI software can work in tandem with a drone's video camera and GPS to help the machine create a real-time map of the ground, stay locked in position, dodge objects like trees and wires, and identify safe landing spots.

Clogging Airspace

Even as manufacturers seek to improve drone capabilities, the machines continue to raise concerns about safety. Drones flown by amateurs have endangered thousands of light aircraft and commercial jets throughout the world. In August 2015 alone there were more than seventy reports of drones interfering with airplanes or coming too close to US airports. Twelve incidents occurred in a single day, affecting flights in Florida, Illinois, New Mexico, North Carolina, and Texas. As reporter Craig Whitlock writes, "Before last year [2014], close encounters with rogue drones were unheard of. But as a result of a sales boom, small, largely unregulated remote-control aircraft are clogging U.S. airspace, snarling air traffic and giving the FAA [Federal Aviation Administration] fits."[4]

The FAA is the government agency that oversees all aspects of civil aviation in the United States, including the use of drones. In 2015 the agency began requiring consumers to pay five dollars to register their drones. Within a year, 400,000 private and commercial drones were registered to operate in American skies; by comparison, there were 590,000 FAA licensed pilots of manned aircraft in the United States in 2016. And according to the FAA, 4.3 million consumer drones and 2.7 million commercial drones could be flying the skies by 2020.

While the FAA struggles to regulate the new technology, the 2010s might be remembered as the beginning of the age of drones. The skies are already buzzing with consumer drones, and artificial intelligence is being applied to machines with the ability to see, hear, and fly. By the end of the 2020s, drones will likely be seen almost everywhere, delivering food, picking up garbage, watching children on the playground, and even transporting passengers. When it comes to the future of drones, it seems only the sky is the limit.

Chapter 1

Drones of War

The militant group al Shabaab has brutally imposed its own strict version of Islamic law on villagers in one African nation after another. In 2013 the group massacred sixty-seven people at a mall in Nairobi, Kenya, and in 2015 al Shabaab fighters slaughtered twenty-five guests staying at a hotel in Somalia's capital, Mogadishu. The US military views al Shabaab as a threat; there are fears al Shabaab might be planning attacks on US military bases in Africa and elsewhere.

In March 2016 about two hundred al Shabaab soldiers were gathered at a training camp north of Mogadishu. US military drones had been monitoring the camp for months. According to US secretary of the air force Deborah Lee James, the drones provided intelligence that indicated "these fighters would soon be embarking upon missions that would directly impact the U.S. and our partners."[5] The air force launched an air strike on the training camp, killing more than 150 al Shabaab soldiers. It was the deadliest attack ever launched against al Shabaab by the United States—and not a single US service member suffered injury. In fact, no US service members were anywhere nearby. Rather, they were about 1,100 miles (1,700 km) away at a US drone air base in Chabelley, Djibouti, where they sat at the controls of several unmanned MQ-9 Reaper drones that carried out the strike.

Joysticks and Missiles

The drone strike in Somalia proved once again the power of drones to monitor enemies unobserved and kill with deadly precision. Drones are equipped with high-tech tools that allow operators to see and hear events on the ground. Pilots view potential targets through high-definition cameras attached to the underside of the craft. Facial recognition software is used to identify targeted individuals. Electronic sensors in drones pick up signals from terrorists' cell phones. These signals identify individuals by the sound of their voice while pinpointing their exact location.

The Pentagon has used its eyes and ears in the sky to exact a heavy toll on enemy targets without endangering US personnel. For this reason the United States has greatly expanded the use of drones since 2005, when the military operated about fifty UAVs in the Iraq War. By 2016 the Pentagon was using an estimated seven thousand UAVs. Most were flown remotely by pilots at Creech Air Force Base outside of Las Vegas, Nevada, and MacDill Air Force Base in Tampa, Florida. The military also wages drone war from bases in Afghanistan, the island nation of Seychelles, and elsewhere.

Two of the military's most valuable drones are the MQ-1 Predator and the MQ-9 Reaper. The Predator is 27 feet (8.2 m) long and can reach speeds of up to 135 miles per hour (217 kph). It can hover over targets for fourteen hours at heights of up to 25,000 feet (7,620 m). The Reaper is 36 feet (11 m) long and has a maximum speed of 300 miles per hour (483 kph). It is among the US military's deadliest weapons. The Reaper can carry four laser-guided supersonic Hellfire missiles. Each missile delivers a 100-pound (45 kg) bomb designed to penetrate bunkers and destroy tanks. The Reaper and Predator are both controlled by joysticks similar to those used in video games.

Deadly Force

Since 2002 the US military has used Predators and Reapers to carry out hundreds of targeted killings inside and outside war zones and conflict areas. Drone attacks have killed Taliban leaders in Pakistan and Afghanistan, Islamic State (ISIS) militants in Syria and Iraq, and al Qaeda forces in Libya, Yemen, and elsewhere. And the use of drones is expanding. In 2015 the Pentagon announced plans to increase the number of drone flights by 50

The MQ-9 Reaper (pictured) can carry four laser-guided Hellfire missiles, each of which delivers enough firepower to penetrate bunkers and destroy tanks. The Reaper is among the US military's deadliest weapons.

percent by 2019. And a new generation of drones currently under development will be more deadly than the last.

The Pentagon is currently working to build autonomous, or self-directed, killer drones. These drones will be equipped with AI that will enable them to hunt for and kill specific human targets. Once the job is complete, the killer drones will return to their home base. As journalist Annie Jacobsen explains: "The nontechnical term for an autonomous drone is a hunter-killer robot, a robotic system 'intelligent' enough to be shown a photograph of a person and told to return when the target has been killed."[6]

The United States is not the only nation developing hunter-killer robots. Scientists in Russia, China, and other nations are also developing drones of all sizes and shapes meant to remove humans from the war-making equation. This has sparked fears among military analysts who envision a day when wars are not fought between humans but by drones programmed with artificial intelligence.

Micro, Bug, and Nano Drones

While the military utilizes large drones that fly high in the sky, researchers are working to significantly shrink drones to kill enemies and aid soldiers on the ground. Tiny drones are known as "micro," "bug," or "nano" drones. In 2016 British soldiers in Afghanistan were testing the Black Hornet Nano. The drone is about 1 by 8 inches (2.6 by 20 cm) and weighs little more than half an ounce (16 grams). The Black Hornet has a single propeller, can reach speeds of 22 miles per hour (35 kph), and can stay aloft for twenty-five minutes. The drone is equipped with three cameras; one points forward, another straight down, and the third downward at a 45-degree angle. A digital link sends high-resolution video and still-camera images to flip-down, chest-mounted screens worn by operators. Most importantly, because it is so small, it can operate without anyone even noticing it.

Images gathered by the Black Hornet allow soldiers to see around corners and over obstacles in order to identify hidden dangers. The drone is also flown into enemy territory to gather intelligence; revealing the strength, position, and movements of adversaries. Commanding officer Major Adam Foden explains the advantages of the bug drone:

[The] Black Hornet is a game-changing piece of [equipment]. Previously, we would have had to send soldiers forward to see if there were any enemy fighters hiding inside a set of buildings. Now we are deploying Black Hornet to look inside compounds and to clear a route through enemy-held spaces. It has worked very well and the pictures it delivers back to the monitor are really clear and Black Hornet is so small and quiet that the locals can't see or hear it.[7]

The Black Hornet can be used to spot a sniper waiting to ambush a squadron or locate booby traps and roadside bombs.

The Black Hornet Nano (foreground) is small but powerful. It can gather crucial intelligence on enemy positions and movements without being noticed and then send information and photos back to its operator.

The clear pictures allow soldiers to distinguish between civilians and militant fighters in ways never before possible. According to Foden, the Black Hornet's camera "can zoom right up to some-body's face and hold that frame for as long as is required so we can identify them without them even knowing it's there."[8]

Autonomous Weapons

Drones of all shapes and sizes are already changing how wars are fought. As dramatic as these changes are, analysts consider this era to be the first age of drone warfare, one in which drones are still controlled by soldiers and used against individual enemies. The second age of drone warfare—if and when it materializes—will utilize AI and likely lead to even greater changes in warfare. Drones equipped with AI might one day be capable of learning the terrain of a battlefield, identifying and killing targets, and even battling other AI drones without human input. Not everyone looks forward to this future. As physicist and AI expert Steve Omohundro explains, "These [autonomous] systems are likely to behave in anti-social and harmful ways unless they are very carefully designed. . . . Fully autonomous weapons threaten to violate the foundational rights to life."[9]

Abilities such as this are still only a distant possibility. AI technology, while advancing, was still fairly primitive in 2016. As director of Facebook AI Research Yann LeCun states: "AIs are nowhere near as smart as a rat."[10] However, researchers at numerous university and tech company laboratories are building AI robots that can teach themselves to walk, talk, and build and sort objects. At Google headquarters in California, artificial intelligence is being put to use in self-driving cars.

Military planners see many advantages in combining AI with drones that already use powerful software to map flight paths, control speed and altitude, and navigate from one point to another without input from operators. That is why Secretary of the Navy Ray Mabus announced in 2015 that the military plans to develop autonomous drone weapons: "Unmanned systems, particularly autonomous ones, have to be the new normal in ever-increasing areas."[11]

Swarm Troopers

The next generation of war-fighting drones will likely be far more sophisticated than the ones used by today's military. The military is building less expensive, disposable drones, referred to by the acronym LAWS (lethal autonomous weapons systems). LAWS are equipped with deadly explosives and operate cooperatively in groups called swarms. A swarm of drones can either be controlled by a single human operator or work autonomously to learn and perform tasks. Tech journalist David Hambling explains the advantages to what he calls swarm troopers:

> A swarm of armed drones is like a flying minefield. The individual elements may not be that dangerous, but they are so numerous that they are impossible to defeat. They can be disabled one by one, but the cumulative risk makes it

safer to avoid them than to try to destroy them all. Mine-fields on land may be avoided; the flying minefield goes anywhere. When it strikes targets on the ground the swarm can overwhelm any existing opposition by sheer numbers of intelligently-targeted warheads.[12]

A navy program called Low-Cost UAV Swarming Technology (LOCUST) was among the first in the world to test swarm troopers. The LOCUST system consists of a device that can launch drones in rapid succession. The launcher is small enough to be mounted on a vehicle and can also be attached to an airplane or ship. The launcher works with small drones such as the Coyote, which is 3 feet (91 cm) long. Coyote drones can be equipped with warheads and fly at speeds approaching 100 miles per hour (161 kph).

Birds, Insects, Canines, and Drones

It is no accident that small drones are named Raven, Black Hornet, and Coyote. The scientists who created them often model their software on the behavior of birds, insects, and canines.

Researchers studied the way geese and other migratory birds fly in V formation. Geese fly this way because it is aerodynamic; the flapping wings of the goose in front create an updraft of air that provides a lift to those flying beside and behind. Scientists estimate that flying in this formation is 70 percent easier than flying alone. The same is true when multiple drones fly in this formation—they use less power to stay in the air.

Researchers also studied how wolves attack their prey. When wolves hunt they work as a pack, circling their prey and spreading out at an equal distance. One wolf after another lunges at the prey, forcing it to turn in circles. The animal eventually gets dizzy, tired, and disoriented, which gives the wolves a chance to close in for the kill. Computer scientist Raymond Coppinger of Hampshire College in Amherst, Massachusetts, created a computer simulation for drones based on the behavior of a wolf pack when attacking a large prey animal. When this pattern is applied to a swarm of small drones, the machines can effectively work together autonomously, without instructions from an operator.

When numerous Coyotes are airborne at once, they communicate with each other and fly to targets in a synchronized V formation, cutting efficiently through the air like a flock of geese. When encountering enemy troops, vehicles, and boats, the autonomous drones drop from the sky to attack like a swarm of insects.

LOCUSTs and CICADAs

In a 2015 demonstration, the navy used the LOCUST system to simultaneously launch thirty Coyotes. According to program manager Lee Mastroianni, "This level of autonomous swarming flight has never been done before. UAVs . . . will free manned aircraft and traditional weapon systems to do more, and essentially multiply combat power at decreased risk to the warfighter."[13]

In a similar, but unrelated, program, the navy is developing drones called Close-In Covert Autonomous Disposable Aircraft (CICADA). These small, unmanned aerial vehicles, or micro drones, fit in the palm of the hand, are undetectable by radar, and contain circuit boards, computer chips, and GPS receivers. They can be created inexpensively with a 3D printer, which makes solid three-dimensional objects from a fine plastic dust called PMMA.

In tests conducted by the US Naval Research Laboratory, hundreds of CICADAs were "seeded," or dropped by a large drone flying at an altitude of 50,000 feet (15,240 meters). The autonomous micro drones avoided cliffs, trees, and other obstacles to land within 15 feet (4.65 meters) of a target.

Naval planners envision various ways of using the CICADA micro drones. One possibility is to drop tens of thousands of them behind enemy lines. Equipped with microphones, they can eavesdrop on enemy troops without anyone ever noticing. CICADAs equipped with magnetic sensors could also be dropped in the ocean to detect the movement of enemy submarines. Yet another scenario involves using swarms of micro drones to deliver payloads, or tiny explosive warheads. Enemy fighters would be unable to defend themselves against thousands of deadly micro drones dropping out of the sky.

Enemy Swarms

Military analysts worry about what might happen if such drones were to fall into enemy hands. A swarm of micro drones, for instance, could overwhelm the air defenses deployed by navy destroyers. American battleships are protected by a high-tech system called Aegis, which is the most advanced and effective defensive system in the world. It can identify, track, and destroy incoming aircraft, missiles, and other threats in seconds. But in tests conducted by naval researchers, Aegis was not effective in fighting what Hambling calls swarming suicide drones:

> The problem was that the suicide drones were so small they were often not detected until they were dangerously close. When they were spotted, the defenses only had a limited time to shoot down several difficult targets. . . . Researchers concluded that with eight drones approaching simultaneously, four could be expected to get through and hit the destroyer. Four small warheads would not sink a destroyer, but they could certainly damage it and cause loss of life.[14]

Suicide drone swarms might kill sailors manning machine guns and could also target radar and missile systems, leaving the ship without defenses. Enemies could then use larger weapons to sink the destroyer. And researchers only conducted simulated tests with a swarm of eight drones. A swarm of fifty would be nearly impossible to stop.

A Glimpse of the Future

While military planners confront the problems associated with swarming enemy drones, another navy program involves teaching drones to perform one of the most dangerous tasks in the military— aircraft carrier landings. Pilots approach aircraft carriers

Sailors move an X-47B Unmanned Combat Air System onto an elevator aboard the aircraft carrier USS George H.W. Bush. *On this day in 2013, the pilotless craft made history when it took off from and landed on an aircraft carrier.*

at speeds of 170 miles per hour (274 kph). The ship pitches and rolls in the waves while moving at 35 miles per hour (56 kph). The plane stops by catching a hook under its belly on a steel arresting cable stretched across the ship's deck.

Military planners are hoping the X-47B Unmanned Combat Air System can eliminate the peril posed by piloted aircraft landings. The X-47B is a 14,000-pound (6,350 kg) autonomous drone with a 62-foot (19 m) wingspan and a range of 2,400 miles (3,862 km). The drone is capable of aerial refueling, meaning it can stay aloft indefinitely. Using advanced flight control software, the X-47B can be used as a bomber or for intelligence, surveillance, and reconnaissance. The only input the drone requires from humans amounts to a few strokes on a computer keyboard.

In 2013 the pilotless X-47B made history when it successfully took off from and landed on an aircraft carrier, the USS *George H.W. Bush*. After the X-47B completed one of aviation's most challenging maneuvers, Mabus heralded the achievement: "It isn't very often you get a glimpse of the future. Today, those of us aboard the USS *George H.W. Bush* got that chance as we witnessed the X-47B make its first-ever . . . landing aboard an aircraft carrier."[15]

Yet another test of the X-47B was conducted in 2014. This one sought to find out if the UAV could operate alongside piloted aircraft. This is important because of the likelihood of UAVs and piloted aircraft working on the same missions. In this test the pilotless X-47B took off and landed in tandem with a piloted F/A-18 Super Hornet jet fighter. The drone had to function flawlessly, including quickly detaching itself from the arrestor wire, or cable, that stretches across the flight deck to stop the plane. The drone then had to fold its wings and safely move out of the way within ninety seconds so the Super Hornet could land. If the drone could not quickly and accurately perform these tasks, it would not be possible to use it alongside manned aircraft. However, the test was a success.

Human-Drone Cyborgs

The navy performs some of the most scientifically advanced drone research in the world. But the Defense Advanced Research Projects Agency (DARPA) is working on weapons systems that will involve an entire army of drones. DARPA is the secretive Pentagon organization that in the past developed everything from the Internet to stealth technology used on military aircraft. In 2015, in addition to building unmanned aerial vehicles, DARPA was working on drone weapons called unmanned ground systems, unmanned surface vehicles, unmanned maritime systems, and unmanned aircraft systems. Depending on the drones, the machines will fly, swim, crawl, walk, and run. DARPA planners hope to use them to wage war from the deepest oceans to outer space.

One DARPA concept, called Augmented Cognition, is based on the science fiction notion of a cyborg, a person with physical abilities extended by mechanical elements built into the body. DARPA wants to use Augmented Cognition to create biohybrids, or human-machine hybrids. Biohybrids would be created by implanting a computer chip in the brain of a human soldier; the chip could exchange information with a drone. The soldier's thoughts would be encoded as electrical impulses and transferred to the drone with Wi-Fi technology. In this scenario, which is under development, a biohybrid soldier would not control a drone with a joystick but with his or her thoughts. In theory, a soldier would also be able to see, hear, and smell information picked up by sensors on a drone.

Gambling on Drone Strikes

Drones are incredibly effective at hitting predetermined targets, and under President Barack Obama the US military has made extensive use of these powerful weapons. The military classifies drone strikes and resulting casualties as top secret information. But in 2015 the *Intercept*, an online publication, received classified military documents that revealed that since 2008 up to 90 percent of those killed in drone strikes—around four thousand people—were civilians. Around nine hundred fatalities were children. Obama has acknowledged that drone strikes kill civilians, despite intelligence on targets being double-checked and triple-checked to avoid such casualties.

The news of civilian deaths has fueled renewed criticism of the drone war by those who believe the missile strikes do more harm than good. Critics point out that when innocent civilians are killed, it fuels widespread feelings of hatred against the United States, and terrorists use civilian deaths as a recruiting tool.

Government officials continue to state that drone strikes are accurate and rarely harm civilians. Humanitarian organizations and some political analysts, however, are deeply troubled by the military's ongoing use of drones. As the anonymous source of the classified documents told the *Intercept*: "Anyone caught in the vicinity [of a drone strike] is guilty by association. [When] a drone strike kills more than one person, there is no guarantee that those persons deserved their fate. . . . So it's a phenomenal gamble."

Quoted in Marina Fang, "Nearly 90 Percent of People Killed in Recent Drone Strikes Were Not the Target," *Huffington Post*, October 20, 2015. www.huffingtonpost.com.

Benefits and Risks

While DARPA scientists meld science with science fiction, critics of military drone programs worry about autonomous machines making targeting decisions. Some even worry that powerful AI cyborgs could turn their deadly weapons on their human controllers. As renowned physicist Stephen Hawking explains: "A superintelligent AI [drone] will be extremely good at accomplishing its goals, and if those goals aren't aligned with ours, we're in trouble."[16]

Some opponents of military drones are urging nations to agree to treaties that ban the robotic machines. But this might not be possible, as computer scientist Pedro Domingos writes:

> Far from banning drones . . . countries large and small are busy developing them, presumably because in their estimation the benefits outweigh the risks. As with any weapon, it's safer to have robots than to trust the other side not to. If in future wars millions of kamikaze drones will destroy conventional armies in minutes, they'd better be our drones. If World War III will be over in seconds, as one side takes control of the other's systems, we'd better have the smarter, faster, more resilient [drone] network.[17]

Whether humans will control drones or drone warfare will take on a life of its own remains an open question. But in little more than a decade, drones have evolved from unmanned airplanes to exotic robots whose war-making potential is only beginning to be understood. And developments in the field seem to be moving faster than the ability to regulate or control the technology. As drones continue to change the rules of the game, it is up to those with their hands on the remote controls to ensure that UAVs are used in ways that help soldiers, deter enemies, and protect the lives of average citizens on the ground.

Chapter 2

Law Enforcement Eyes in the Sky

Every spring about seventy-five thousand college students stream into the resort town of South Padre Island, Texas, to celebrate spring break. And every year local police rescue swimmers in distress, break up fights, and arrest hundreds of partiers for underage drinking, public intoxication, and illegal drug use. In March 2016 South Padre Island police added new tools to maintain security: two Yuneec Typhoon Q500 drones with high-resolution cameras and batteries that provide up to twenty-five minutes of flight time.

During spring break the police drones hovered 250 feet (76 m) above local beaches and allowed officers to keep watch and act effectively in case of trouble. As South Padre Island town spokesperson Gary Ainsworth explained, "It gives us a bird's-eye view that we wouldn't have before. If you have an incident in a large crowd and you're sending two officers into the middle of it, they're vastly outnumbered, and that's before they have any idea of what's going on."[18] Ainsworth also said each drone was equipped to perform rescue missions: The machines could fly out over the water and drop a life jacket near a drowning person.

A Drone's Unblinking Eye

Since 2012 government agencies have been allowed to use small drones—those weighing less than 55 pounds (25 kg)—after obtaining a certificate from the FAA. According to the digital rights organization Electronic Frontier Foundation, at least twenty-four police agencies across the United States are using drones to enhance common police activities. In 2016 drones were being used for surveillance, crime prevention, criminal apprehension, and search-and-rescue missions in Alabama, Arkansas, Florida, North Dakota, Texas, Utah, and elsewhere. Drones were also being deployed by federal agencies, including the FBI, US Border Patrol, and National Park Service. The unmanned aircraft cost $15,000 to $50,000 each, far less than police helicopters, which can cost $500,000 to $3 million each.

Police drones can be equipped with extremely high-resolution cameras that can obtain detailed photographs of people, homes, terrain, and even small objects like a gun. Police drones are also equipped with GPS and heat sensors that can track a person's movements in light or dark conditions. License plate readers on drones can single out cars on the highway. The information is sent in real time to law enforcement officials.

In the coming years police drones might be equipped with facial recognition software that will access the FBI's Next Generation

Officers with the Michigan State Police have been training with this UAV. It carries an infrared camera that enables police to see activity taking place on the ground.

Identification database, which contains photographic information on at least 52 million Americans. This will make it possible to remotely identify people in parks, in schools, and at political gatherings. According to senior national securities strategist Douglas C. Lovelace, a fully equipped police drone will "enable the tracking of as many as 65 different targets across a distance of 65 square miles. . . . That would make it possible to remotely identify individuals subject to a drone's unblinking eye virtually anywhere at any time."[19]

Drones on US Borders

The Border Patrol relies on the unblinking eyes of drones to detect illegal immigrants and drug smugglers along US borders with both Canada and Mexico. The Border Patrol operates eight Predator drones on the country's northern border and ten Predators on the southern border. On occasion, Border Patrol drones have been used for other purposes, such as helping local law enforcement agencies. This happened in 2011, when a Border Patrol drone was used to assist local police in an armed standoff. The problem began when North Dakota cattle rancher Rodney Brossart refused to release six of his neighbor's cows that had wandered onto his ranch. The neighbor called police to get his cows back, but Brossart and his three sons, all armed with rifles, refused to let authorities onto the property. A SWAT team was called in, leading to a sixteen-hour armed standoff.

Police requested help from the Border Patrol, which used the Predator to conduct overnight surveillance and take photos of the Brossarts and their ranch. The police were alerted when the Brossarts were seen outside without their weapons. Brossart and his sons were arrested, and the cows were returned to the neighbor. In 2014 Brossart was convicted of terrorizing police and sentenced to six months in prison; his sons each received a year's probation.

Adopting Drone Laws

Lawmakers in some states have adopted laws that both expand and clarify appropriate use of drones by law enforcement. In

Police Drones and Privacy

The Fourth Amendment to the US Constitution states: "The right of the people to be secure in their persons, houses, papers, and effects, against unreasonable searches and seizures, shall not be violated . . . but upon probable cause." This means that government authorities cannot intrude into people's private lives without a warrant issued by a judge based on the reasonable suspicion of criminal activity. However, when police fly drones over homes, businesses, and public places like sidewalks and parks, the majority of people being observed and photographed are innocent citizens. Most police departments are sensitive to this issue, and in 2012 the International Association of Chiefs of Police issued guidelines for the use of unmanned aircraft (UA) in law enforcement. Among the recommendations:

> The [police] agency should assure the community that it values the protections provided citizens by the U.S. Constitution. Further, that the agency will operate the aircraft in full compliance with the mandates of the Constitution, federal, state and local law governing search and seizure. . . .
>
> Equipping the aircraft with weapons of any type is strongly discouraged. . . .
>
> Where there are specific . . . grounds to believe that the UA will collect evidence of criminal wrongdoing and if the UA will intrude upon reasonable expectations of privacy, the agency will secure a search warrant prior to conducting the flight. . . .
>
> Unless required as evidence of a crime, as part of an on-going investigation, for training, or required by law, images captured by a UA should not be retained by the agency.

International Association of Chiefs of Police Aviation Committee, "Recommended Guidelines for the Use of Unmanned Aircraft," August 2012. www.theiacp.org.

2015, for instance, North Dakota became the first state to legalize weaponized drones for law enforcement purposes. The law allows small drones to be equipped with nonlethal weapons such as rubber bullets, Tasers, pepper spray, and tear gas. However, in the year following the law's passage, no police agencies had yet equipped their drones with such weapons.

Some cities are legalizing non-weaponized drones but only for use in specific situations. In 2015 lawmakers in San Jose,

California, approved the use of police drones in cases where there is an active shooter. A camera on a drone can provide the location of a shooter, which in turn allows police to alert and move people who might be in the area. While no drones have been used in San Jose since the law's passage, security analyst Sean Varah explains the advantages of drones in active shooter situations. He says that drones "can be deployed from almost anywhere and stored in the trunk of a cruiser. They can also access areas traditional helicopters cannot.

UAVs have an ability to fly lower to the ground, get into tight spots, hover under bridges and structures, and even fly inside buildings in order to help the experts gather as much detail as they can."[20]

An Investigative Tool

The ability to fly, hover, and gather details could make drones important tools for another branch of law enforcement: forensic photographers. Forensic photographers collect and analyze crime scene evidence. They visually record the scene from every conceivable angle before the site is cleaned up. The photographs are viewed by detectives working to solve the crime and by lawyers, judges, and juries to either exonerate or convict suspects.

Forensic photographers work slowly and methodically; it can take hours, or even days, to provide a full photographic record of a crime scene. When the setting is indoors, this might not be a problem, but when the crime took place outdoors, time may become an issue. Weather conditions such as rain, wind, cold, and heat can taint or even destroy evidence.

Aided by a drone, however, a forensic photographer could fully document a crime scene in a much shorter span of time. Sensors in the drone could mark evidence with precise ground measurements. Cameras aboard the drone could capture video and 3D still images for later use by investigators as they reconstruct the crime.

The accuracy and convenience of drones prompted police in Winnipeg, Canada, to purchase eight drones in 2014 to take aerial photos and videos of crime scenes. Winnipeg police corporal Byron Charbonneau explains the advantages of drones:

> Particularly when you have an outdoor crime scene, timeliness is of importance. The problem we run into when we're using conventional aircraft, is you can't always get an aircraft there in a timely fashion. It could be days. . . . We can deploy the UAV almost immediately to get the aerial photographs while the evidence is still present, while it's unaltered. If we have to wait a couple of days to get aerial evidence and it rains or it snows, that's a problem.[21]

Search and Rescue

One of the most promising fields for drones in police work involves search-and-rescue missions. Thousands of search-and-rescue operations are coordinated by local, county, state, and federal agencies every year. The missions are conducted at sea, in rural and wilderness areas, and in towns and cities throughout the world. Search-and-rescue personnel are deployed to find lost hikers, missing crime victims, people involved in air and water accidents, and those who disappear in snowstorms, floods, tornadoes, and earthquakes.

In 2016 Canadian search-and-rescue teams were experimenting with drones in British Columbia. The drones can fly at night over rugged terrain, map out search areas to aid response teams, and home in on the body heat of lost individuals. There is one major obstacle in using drones for wilderness search-and-rescue missions; the machines cannot fly autonomously in complex environments like a dense forest. A slight error like hitting a tree branch can cause the drone to crash.

In 2016 a team of Swiss scientists headed by robotics expert Davide Scaramuzza developed powerful software to help drones equipped with four rotors, called quadcopters, navigate in forests and other complex environments. According to Scaramuzza,

WORDS IN CONTEXT

forensic
Relating to the application of scientific methods and techniques to the investigation of crime.

A member of an Alaskan search-and-rescue team checks his map after a briefing about a missing hiker. Some teams are experimenting with drones for mapping search areas and locating heat signatures from lost individuals.

"We've created artificial intelligence software to teach a small quadcopter to autonomously recognize and follow forest trails. It's a first in the fields of artificial intelligence and robotics. This success means drones could soon be used in parallel with rescue teams to accelerate the search for people lost in the wilderness."[22]

Like other drones, the search-and-rescue machine sees the forest though a pair of small cameras. But the drone does not rely on sensors alone to dodge trees and other objects. Instead it uses a powerful AI program that teaches the drone to recognize existing trails. Scaramuzza explains how the drone was taught to perform this task: "We first made our drone 'watch' as many images of forest trails as possible. The effort paid off: when tested on a new, previously unseen trail, the [AI] network was able to find the correct direction in 85 percent of cases. In comparison, humans faced with the same task guessed correctly 82 percent of the time."[23]

Scaramuzza points out that in Switzerland alone, about one thousand lost or injured hikers need to be rescued every year. He says dozens of drones equipped with his software could be deployed at once, reducing response time when emergencies occur. But work is not finished on the software; the scientists hope to make it function in the dark.

Protecting Wildlife

Drones can also be used to stop illegal poaching in wilderness areas. About twelve hundred endangered rhinos are killed in South Africa every year by poachers who sell the animals' horns. Rhino horns can fetch up to $500,000 each in Asia and Africa, where people believe—wrongly—that the horns have medicinal properties. Elephants are also vulnerable to poaching. Thirty thousand elephants are killed annually in South Africa, where a pair of ivory tusks—highly prized as a material for making art objects—can fetch up to $125,000.

The Institute for Advanced Computer Studies at the University of Maryland has used drones to track poachers in South Africa since 2013. Over time, experts have learned a lot about where and when poachers strike. According to Thomas Snitch, a computer professor at the institute, a large percentage of poaching takes place on nights around the full moon, when poachers can see their prey. Rhinos and elephants are most often killed right after sunset, between six and eight o'clock in the evening. Additionally, most poachers work within 525 feet (160 m) of a road so they can quickly escape after killing the animal. Other analytical data compiled by the institute includes information about weather, moon phases, past poaching locations, and movements of rhinos and elephants based on the ankle monitors worn by the animals.

White rhinos (pictured) are an endangered species. Authorities in South Africa are successfully using drones to track and stop poachers, who represent one of the biggest threats to the rhino population.

This data allows authorities to predict with 90 percent certainty where and when rhinos and elephants will be killed.

Although the information compiled by the Institute for Advanced Computer Studies helps law enforcement officials understand where poachers might strike, rhinos and elephants roam over huge areas. For example, South Africa's Kruger National Park is the size of New Jersey. This is where drones proved their worth; using institute data, UAVs are being employed to patrol in places poachers are expected, as Snitch explains:

> On our first UAV flight in South Africa [in May 2013], the UAV flew to our pre-determined spot and immediately found a female rhino and her calf; they were within 30 meters of a major road. We decided to circle the drone over the rhinos, and within minutes a vehicle stopped at the park's fence. Three individuals exited the car and began to climb the fence to kill the rhinos. Our rangers had been

pre-deployed to the area; they arrested the three poachers in less than three minutes.[24]

Snitch says that the same scenario was repeated twenty times during the two years that followed. The poachers who are captured are prosecuted to the fullest extent of the law. And the drones changed the behavior of prospective poachers who fear apprehension; in areas where drones are deployed, poaching has come to a complete halt.

Mixed Views About Drones

Although the use of drones by law enforcement agencies worldwide is increasing, the public has mixed feelings about them. A 2015 Reuters poll found that 68 percent of Americans support police use of drones for solving crimes; 62 percent support routine surveillance by drones equipped with cameras; and 88 percent favor the use of drones for search-and-rescue missions. However, a recent poll conducted by the Associated Press reveals that many Americans have concerns about routine police surveillance of law-abiding citizens. In that poll, one-third of respondents said they fear police use of drones will lead to an erosion of privacy. California senator Dianne Feinstein addressed the issue during a 2013 Senate Judiciary Committee investigation into drone surveillance: "I think the greatest threat to the privacy of Americans is the drone and the use of the drone, and the very few regulations that are on it today."[25]

The reason law enforcement authorities are generally free to use drones goes back to a 1986 US Supreme Court decision. In that case, the court ruled that warrantless aerial observation of a backyard did not violate a person's constitutional right to privacy. According to the court, a person who is outdoors should expect to be observed by anyone, including police.

The fear that drones are violating privacy rights has nevertheless created an anti-drone backlash in some places. Since 2013 lawmakers in Seattle, Washington; Tallahassee, Florida; and Charlottesville, Virginia, have banned the use of drones for police work. In addition, Illinois, North Carolina, Utah, and several other states

Criminals Using Drones

Law enforcement agencies are not alone in finding new uses for drones. Drones have also become a favorite of lawbreakers. In 2014 prison officials in South Carolina discovered a drone carrying contraband, including marijuana and a mobile phone, into the yard at the Lee Correctional Institution in Bishopville. And in 2015 several ounces of marijuana and a quarter ounce of heroin was successfully delivered by drone into the prison yard at the Mansfield Correctional Institution in Ohio. (Authorities confiscated the package after a brawl erupted among inmates fighting over the delivery.)

Drugs are also being flown across US borders by drug dealers in Mexico. Since 2012 the Drug Enforcement Administration has traced at least 150 flights of what it calls narco drones crossing the border. In one instance, a drug gang operating near Mexico City hired aircraft factory workers to assemble drones much larger than an average consumer drone. The drones, which were capable of flying low and undetected by radar, could each carry 200 pounds (91 kg) of cocaine.

There are also fears that terrorists might use drones to inflict mass casualties. In 2016 a team of British intelligence analysts drew up a scenario in which a swarm of bomb-equipped drones was launched by terrorists at a major sporting event like the Super Bowl. The analysts noted that a single drone could carry about 20 pounds (9 kg) of TNT, roughly equivalent to the amount in an explosive vest worn by a suicide bomber. A mass drone attack would be similar to dozens of suicide bombers simultaneously detonating their vests.

have enacted bills requiring police to obtain a search warrant from a judge before using a drone to observe a suspect in a crime.

However, local and state laws do not prevent federal agencies like the US Department of Justice (DOJ) from conducting drone surveillance. And the DOJ—which oversees the FBI, the Drug Enforcement Administration, and other enforcement agencies—has assembled a large domestic fleet of Predators and other drones. The Electronic Frontier Foundation found that DOJ drones flew more than seven hundred missions from 2010 to 2012 for federal agencies and local police departments. In 2015 it was revealed that the FBI alone flew drones above more than thirty cities in eleven states across the country. The drones took photos and videos and were also equipped with technology that could identify thousands of people below through the cell phones they carry. The Predators were also furnished with Vehicle and Dismount Exploitation Radar, developed by the military to detect and follow insurgents in Afghanistan. Defense and national security expert Michael Peck explains why some are concerned about this development: "Drones are relatively cheap and can be equipped with sophisticated sensors, so they can vacuum up large amounts of camera imagery and other data. . . . It is not clear what police are doing with the data. So we could face a future where the skies are crisscrossed by police drones tracking suspected criminals, and in the process, spying on the rest of us."[26] After news of the FBI drone program appeared in the media, bureau spokesperson Christopher Allen issued a statement meant to calm the fears of privacy rights advocates: "[FBI planes] are not equipped, designed or used for bulk collection activities or mass surveillance."[27]

Lawbreakers and Law Enforcers

While the debate ensues over the use of drones to prevent crimes, criminals are exploiting weaknesses in drones used by the government. In January 2016 the DHS reported that Mexican drug traffickers had hacked into the GPS that guides US Border Patrol drones. This enabled the hackers to insert fake coordinates into the GPS, which steered the drones away from their designated patrol areas along the Texas border. When the drones were gone, the traffickers were safely able to cross the border with their loads of drugs.

The clash between lawbreakers and law enforcers is nearly as old as civilization. And as the situation along the border demonstrates, technology can be useful to those on both sides of the law. While no one knows what role surveillance drones will play in the future, there is little doubt that the number of law enforcement eyes in the sky will continue to multiply as long as criminals continue to commit crimes.

Chapter 3

The Business of Drones

For many people who live in Minnesota, wintertime means ice fishing. On any given winter weekend, Mille Lacs Lake in central Minnesota attracts hundreds of ice fishers trying their luck. Many will drink a beer or two as they sit in their warm fishing cabins waiting for the fish to bite. In February 2014 a beer company called Lakemaid saw an opportunity in this annual pastime. The company tested a six-rotor drone capable of delivering twelve-packs of beer to ice fishers who did not want to trudge to shore to stock up. After the tests, Lakemaid president Jack Supple explained: "The ability of the UAV to set the twelve pack gently and tenderly down in the snow next to the fish house make us fans of this form of delivery."[28]

Lakemaid shot a video of the company's drone deliveries and proudly posted it on YouTube. The video attracted widespread positive attention from viewers and tech reporters. It also caught the eye of the FAA, which informed Supple that he was in violation of agency regulations. He was ordered to immediately stop using drones for deliveries because, as the FAA noted, the agency did not yet have rules in place for this type of activity.

Amazon Prime Air

The FAA sent Jeff Bezos a similar letter. Bezos is the founder and CEO of Amazon, the world's largest online shopping site. In December 2013 Bezos announced the creation of Amazon Prime Air, which planned to deliver customer packages by drone within thirty minutes of ordering. According to Bezos, 86 percent of Amazon packages weigh less than 5 pounds (2.3 kg) and could easily be delivered by drones at speeds of 50 miles per hour (80 kph). But, like Supple, Bezos discovered that the commercial use

Representatives of Amazon Prime Air demonstrate a prototype of the company's delivery drone. Amazon founder Jeff Bezos believes that delivery drones will one day be a familiar sight in US cities and towns.

of drones was not permitted in the United States at that time.

Bezos hired numerous lawyers and lobbyists to petition Congress and the FAA to change the rules on drone delivery. The agency began granting exemptions in September 2014. To obtain an exemption, a person or company must demonstrate that the drone will not create a hazard to the public or airplanes or pose a threat to national security. Drone operators need to obtain a special pilot's license, which must be renewed every two years. Among other rules, drones can only fly during the day, must remain below 500 feet (152 m), and have to be in the operator's line of sight at all times.

By the end of 2015 fourteen hundred businesses had been granted exemptions to use drones for commercial purposes. One of those businesses was Amazon—but it had a serious problem with the line-of-sight rule. That rule made it nearly impossible to deliver packages over long distances. Frustrated, Bezos's company tested drone delivery in Canada, the United Kingdom, and Netherlands—all of which have fewer restrictions. Bezos believes his company will eventually prevail in the United States. "One day," he says, "Prime Air deliveries will be as common as seeing a mail truck."[29]

"An Economic Game-Changer"

If Bezos is correct, Amazon will be one of thousands of businesses working to incorporate drones into their operations. As this takes place, other changes are likely—including the creation of new jobs. According to Consumer Electronics Association CEO Gary Shapiro, "Unmanned vehicles have the potential to create new businesses and new jobs and give consumers unprecedented remote access to our skies. . . . In short, drones are not just for fun, they are an economic game-changer—one that will transform the way we do business."[30] The business group Association for Unmanned Vehicle Systems International backs up Shapiro's forecast. The association predicts that once the FAA approves the widespread commercial use of drones, one hundred thousand new drone jobs will be created within

Amazon Drones

In 2016 Amazon was working to build and test drones at a rural testing ground outside the small town of Snoqualmie, Washington. Amazon engineers were customizing the drones to perform specialized package delivery tasks. For example, some Amazon drones are being designed to fly in hot, dusty Arizona, while others are meant to fly in cold, snowy Minnesota. Delivery drones also have to be capable of getting their packages to customers in all different types of buildings, including farmhouses, suburban ranch homes, and high-rise apartments in big cities. And the drones have to be built with safety in mind, as Amazon's vice president for global public policy, Paul Misener, explains:

> These are quite different than the drones that you can buy in a store and fly around. These are highly automated drones. They have what is called sense-and-avoid technology. That means, basically, seeing and then avoiding obstacles. . . . The automation technologies already exist. We're making sure that it works, and we have to get to a point where we can demonstrate that [the drones] operate safely.

Quoted in David Pogue, "Exclusive: Amazon Reveals Details About Its Crazy Drone Delivery Program," Yahoo!, January 18, 2016. www.yahoo.com.

ten years. The association says this will amount to an $82 billion economic impact.

Thanks to Amazon, the most high-profile new drone jobs will likely be in customer fulfillment, which involves delivery of items ordered by customers. As drone technology advances and the FAA adapts its rules to the changes, drone operators may be charged with delivering takeout food, groceries, drugs from pharmacies, clothing, toys, books, and even organs for transplants.

WORDS IN CONTEXT

geotag
A function whereby a GPS-enabled device inserts data with geographical information into a file such as photo, associating it with the geographic location it was taken in.

Drone operators who deliver light packages might be thought of as the bike messengers of the future. Other drone operators will be more like long-haul truck drivers, flying large heavy drones laden with packages between distant warehouses. Others might work in drone security, patrolling sprawling commercial properties that contain factories, storage depots, office parks, loading docks, power plants, and parking lots.

Drones could be useful in other fields as well. Photographers, for instance, could benefit from drones that allow them to take overhead photos and videos of weddings. Or real estate agents may want to hire drone photographers to shoot their properties from the air. Even coverage of sporting events could be handled by drone operators.

As with any other piece of specialized technology, drones will likely spawn a large research and development industry. An increasing number of drone entrepreneurs will work in the business of developing drone operating systems and apps. Others could devote themselves to improving flight times and payload capacities, building cheaper hardware, and repairing customized rigs.

Drones on Farms and Ranches

Another area where drone technology is likely to make a big difference is agriculture. The Association for Unmanned Vehicle Systems International estimates that 80 percent of the commercial market for drones in the coming decade will be related to farming and ranching. Farm drones will aid in the task of field inspection, where farmers walk their fields and study the soil and plants. Visual inspections allow a grower to determine proper levels of fertilizer, water, and chemicals such as pesticides and herbicides. Some farmers, particularly those with very large farms, already use photos of their fields taken from manned aircraft or satellites. However, these photos, shot from high in the sky, are expensive to produce and are not the best quality. Low-flying drones with high-definition cameras can eliminate these costly methods and provide much better data for field inspection.

When a drone flies back and forth across a farm field, it can take thousands of photos. Each one has a geotag, an electronic tag that assigns the photo a specific geographical location. Once the flight is finished, the geotagged photos can be assembled into extremely accurate two-dimensional or three-dimensional maps that show exactly where there are problems in the field. With the

Farmers are finding uses for camera-mounted drones similar to the one shown here. Photos taken by drones enable farmers to identify specific water and fertilizer needs for particular crops.

highly specific data, farmers can practice what is called precision agriculture, tailoring their use of fertilizer, water, and chemicals on the basis of how much is needed in a specific place. This saves money by reducing the unnecessary use of chemicals.

Agriculture professor Kevin Price was so excited about the possibilities of precision drone agriculture that he quit his job at Kansas State University to join the Denver company RoboFlight. The Denver-based company sells drones and analyzes the data collected on corn, soybean, and other field crops. Companies like RoboFlight are creating jobs in a new field called aerial agriculture. Experts in this field will create and analyze geotagged photos and gather other information by drone to check on crop health, identify weeds and insects, and devise precision methods for applying fertilizer, pesticides, and water. According to Price, "It is endless right now, the applications in agriculture. . . . [Farmers] are going to be able to see things and monitor their crops in ways they never have before. In the next 10 years almost every farm will be using it."[31]

Pipelines and Power Lines

The utility business is another area of growth for drones and drone employment. Utility companies own gas pipelines, power lines, transformers, transmission towers, solar energy farms, and wind turbines. The companies spend millions of dollars to inspect lines,

WORDS IN CONTEXT

lidar
A combination of the words *light* and *radar*, defining a type of surveying technology that employs laser light to illuminate a target and accurately measure distances.

which can run for hundreds of miles through extremely remote areas. When power lines snap or transformers explode, utility line workers are assigned the dangerous job of examining and repairing the equipment. An average of seventeen utility workers are killed every year by falls and other accidents.

One of the most hazardous utility jobs involves the inspection of the huge blades of wind turbines, which can be more than 200 feet (61 m) off the ground. Consumers Energy executive Andrew Bordine explains how drones can improve worker safety while

Wind turbine inspections can be dangerous because the blades are so high off the ground. Drones offer a safer alternative by allowing inspectors to check the condition of the blades without having to climb on the turbines.

saving money: "With wind turbines, you'll have a couple of guys hanging off the blades by a rope a couple hundred feet in the air to do inspections visually, at a cost upwards of $10,000 per site. We can get the same results with a UAV for $300, without putting workers in danger."[32]

In 2015 Consumers Energy began testing eight-rotor drones in Michigan. The craft were equipped with lidar, a technology used in self-driving cars that measures distances by illuminating targets with laser lights. The energy company is using drone lidar to map and measure its wires and other electrical systems.

Pipeline companies and oil and gas producers are also turning to drones. In 2015 energy giant BP was one of the first oil companies to obtain an exemption for commercial drone use. BP conducted its first drone inspection in Alaska with a 13-pound (6 kg) fixed-wing craft equipped with lidar and 3D sensors. The drone was able to soar over ice floes, flooded fields, and other obstacles to scan pipelines for frost damage, corrosion, and other problems.

In 2016 the oil company Shell Global was using drones in Norway to inspect the tall towers called flare stacks, which burn off flammable gas at refineries. The stacks are 230 feet (70 m) high and were formerly inspected by workers who rappelled down the towers with long ropes. When using workers, Shell had to shut the plant down for nearly two weeks to conduct the inspections. With drones, the inspection takes a few hours and the plant continues with its operations.

Shell also employs drones to inspect the undersides of offshore oil rigs in the North Sea. Because drones are easy and inexpensive to operate, Shell says it can conduct inspections more often, which helps ensure that equipment is performing safely and efficiently at all times.

In addition to saving money and lives, the utility industry is already creating new drone jobs. The companies are hiring pilots and support staff to examine industrial infrastructure like power plants, refineries, roads and rails, shipping terminals, and any other equipment that needs to be scrutinized regularly or closely over time. On the tech side, drone businesses are employing experts to improve the memory and processing power needed to collect large amounts of data in the field. As drone business analyst Maryanna Saenko wrote in 2015, "The [employment] opportunities are in the billions—with a B."[33] In the wind industry alone, Saenko adds, drone sales and service could hit $6 billion by 2024.

Facebook Drones

Facebook cofounder Mark Zuckerberg believes that Internet access is as necessary as pipelines and power lines when it comes to advancing opportunities around the globe. Zuckerberg thinks

Drones, Lasers, and the Internet

Facebook cofounder Mark Zuckerberg believes that nearly every person in the world should be able to access the Internet through a system of solar-powered drones, which will beam the Internet down to earth from high in the sky. As part of this plan, Zuckerberg is pushing to develop a futuristic network that can carry high-capacity Internet connections over long distances. The free space optical (FSO) communications system consists of lasers, invisible beams of light that can transmit data from drones at speeds ten times faster than typical 4G cellular networks.

While an FSO system may work in theory, there is one major problem that needs to be overcome; lasers have to be aimed with incredible accuracy. Zuckerberg compares the task with hitting the Statue of Liberty in New York with a beam of light sent from California, a distance of more than 2,900 miles (4,667 km). Another problem is that an optical laser will not pass through clouds. While Zuckerberg is famous for launching Facebook from his Harvard dorm room in 2004, beaming the Internet from drones using optical lasers is much more difficult. According to Yael Maguire, who is in charge of making FSO a reality: "We're trying to get Mark to understand: This isn't writing code on a laptop and copying it over to a server. There's, like, physical stuff. There's chips and radios and high-powered lasers and [drones] that could fall out of the sky."

Quoted in Jessi Hempel, "Inside Facebook's Ambitious Plan to Connect the Whole World," *Wired*, January 19, 2016. www.wired.com.

that Internet access is necessary to provide a foundation for what he calls the knowledge economy. By boosting Internet connectivity, people will be able find jobs, start companies, challenge government policies, and access health care, education, and financial services. But according to Zuckerberg, only one-third of the world's population has Internet access. He says that providing the other two-thirds of earth's people with connectivity is one of the greatest "challenges of our generation."[34]

Zuckerberg believes that drones are the key to meeting that challenge. According to Zuckerberg, a single drone could beam an Internet signal over a city-sized area of rural territory: "With the efficiency and endurance of high altitude drones, it's even possible that the aircraft could remain aloft for months or years. . . . And unlike satellites, drones don't burn up in the atmosphere when their mission is complete. Instead, they can be easily returned to Earth for maintenance and redeployment."[35]

A whole army of drones could potentially bring connectivity to people worldwide. Toward that end, Zuckerberg has founded an endeavor called Internet.org. One part of Internet.org is a project called the Connectivity Lab. The lab is focused on providing connectivity to those people who cannot access the Internet through cell phones because they live in some of the most remote places on earth.

In 2015 the Connectivity Lab revealed a prototype drone designed to deliver universal connectivity. The fixed-wing Aquila has a wingspan of almost 95 feet (29 m), the same as a Boeing 737 passenger jet, but weighs only about 1,000 pounds (454 kg). The Aquila is solar powered and fitted with batteries so it can stay in the air for up to three months.

The Aquila hovers at altitudes between 60,000 and 90,000 feet (18,288 and 27,432 m) and beams down cellular radio signals carrying the Internet to people living within a 30-mile (48 km) radius. On the ground the signal is distributed as Wi-Fi by cell phones through a network of small cellular towers and satellite dishes. Zuckerberg is also promoting advanced research to move beyond Wi-Fi and cell towers. He believes that special lasers might someday transmit data from drones at speeds much faster than today's cellular networks.

While Zuckerberg works to connect the world through Internet drones, other commercial uses are just over the horizon. And as the little machines with big capabilities take to the skies, they will change the way goods are delivered, crops are grown, and utilities are inspected. Drones are poised to transform industries and employment, and there is little doubt that a technical revolution is in the air.

Chapter 4

Entertainment, News, and Sports

The opening scene of the 2015 movie *The Expendables 3* shows a helicopter chasing a speeding train in a hail of gunfire and explosions. As the heroes in the helicopter engage in a firefight with the bad guys on the train, viewers are treated to a swooping bird's-eye-view of the scene. This was filmed with the help of a drone piloted by Ziv Marom, founder of the media and video production company ZM Interactive.

Producers of action movies like *The Expendables 3* try to outdo each other to create unique and exciting opening scenes. In earlier films a scene like that would have been shot from a helicopter. This would have meant two helicopters and two helicopter crews operating in the same airspace—a hazardous situation at best. Filming with a drone not only eliminates risks to the camera crew but allows producers to capture scenes that would otherwise be impossible. As Marom explains, "We flew right next to a train and helicopter. We shot everything from chasing tanks to explosions to flying over buildings and motorcycle jumps. We can also do shots that a real helicopter can't do. We can do lower altitudes . . . flying in different locations, over the ocean, mountains, rivers, inside buildings, achieving challenging scenes."[36]

The opening shot of *The Expendables 3* was among the most expensive and complex scenes ever shot with a drone. But the distinctive angles of the shot offered audiences direct and instant involvement in the movie. Because of this immediacy, drones are becoming as important to moviemakers as lights and costumes. In recent years drones have been used in several dozen blockbuster films, including the thriller *Eye in the Sky*, the science fiction film *Chappie*, the action movie *Furious 7*, the James Bond film *Spectre*, and the superhero picture *X-Men: Days of Future Past*.

New Rules

Blockbuster films are shot at various locations around the world, but Hollywood remains at the center of the entertainment industry. And 2015 was the first year drones were used on Hollywood film and television shoots. At least sixty productions took advantage of new government rules concerning drones in the entertainment industry. Until 2014 the FAA had banned the use of drones in filmmaking and other commercial endeavors. The agency viewed drones as potential aviation safety hazards and threats to national security. While those worries remained, the Motion Picture Association of America, a film industry trade group, lobbied the FAA to allow the use of drones to capture high-flying aerial footage for entertainment purposes.

Striking Patterns Seen from Above

When the New York City Drone Film Festival handed out awards in 2015, the music video "I Won't Let You Down" by the alternative pop band OK Go won first place in the X Factor category. This category was reserved for drone videos that did not fit into typical groupings such as Landscape, Technical, or Extreme Sports.

The video opens with the band seated on motorized Honda unicycles, spinning on a soundstage in synchronized patterns. A drone delivers shots of band members as they ride outside and through hundreds of elaborately choreographed Japanese schoolgirls spinning umbrellas in scenes resembling views through a kaleidoscope. The camera provides a dizzying drone's-eye-view of the band. The final shot features about fourteen hundred dancers opening and closing umbrellas in unison while moving into various elaborate patterns with military precision.

"I Won't Let You Down" consists of one continuous drone shot that required forty-four takes to capture correctly. The finished video is double time—it is sped up to twice the actual speed of the original shot. The final shot was taken from an altitude of nearly half a mile (800 m). After it was released in October 2014, "I Won't Let You Down" went viral, eventually attracting about 28 million views on YouTube. As festival founder Randy Scott Slavin states, the OK Go video is an example of "what's really possible with drone cinematography."

Quoted in Angela Watercutter, "Drones Are About to Change How Directors Make Movies," *Wired*, March 6, 2015. www.wired.com.

In late 2014 a Carlsbad, California, film company called Aerial MOB was the first production company to receive an FAA exemption to use drones in a Hollywood production. Three months later an Aerial MOB pilot flew a drone on a film set for the first time in the United States, shooting a scene for the TV show *The Mentalist*, which aired in February 2015. The twenty-second shot shows FBI agents gathered at a crime scene near the edge of a forest. The drone takes the camera above the agents, over some trees, and focuses down on the suspected killer who is running away.

To shoot the scene, Aerial MOB had to adhere to strict rules that apply to all film shoots. According to the FAA, drones can be used only during the day on sets that are closed to the public. Operators must hold a recreational or sports pilot certificate. When filming, at least two people are required for drone operation: one to pilot the craft and a second to operate the camera. Most producers also use spotters who watch the drone in flight.

Filmmaking Heroes

The increasing number of drones being used by the entertainment industry follows improvements in cameras, which have gotten smaller and lighter in the past decade even as image quality has improved significantly. The popular GoPro digital camera is at the center of this evolution. GoPros were first introduced in 2006, long before drones captured the public imagination. The little cameras were originally designed as consumer photography products that could be attached to bikes, vehicles, helmets, surfboards, wristbands, and chest harnesses.

While fundamentally changing the way audiences interact with extreme sports, GoPros also transformed cinematography. By 2009 the best-selling GoPro retailer in the United States was an auto parts store located near Universal Studios Hollywood. When GoPro sales executives looked into the phenomenon, they discovered that professional filmmakers were buying GoPro Hero cameras to provide unique shots in car chases and

A snowboarder wears a GoPro camera attached to his helmet. Some moviemakers are getting unique views of car chases and other scenes in their films by using GoPro cameras mounted on drones.

other scenes where large cameras could not be used.

GoPro continued to perfect the Hero. When the company introduced the Hero 4 in 2014, the camera had 4K capabilities. This means it can produce footage known as Ultra High Definition, or Ultra HD. The term *4K* refers to the number of pixels captured by a camera or projected onto a screen. Pixels are tiny electronic dots of light; each pixel contains specific digital information that defines its color and brightness. Whereas an HD image—on a typical modern TV for example—has 1,080 pixels per inch, a 4K image has around 4,000 pixels per inch. This means a 4K picture has four times more definition, making it noticeably brighter and more colorful.

When a GoPro Hero 4 is attached to a drone, moviegoers can see crisp, clear, eye-in-the-sky scenes that were impossible to shoot only a few years ago. And filmmakers with low budgets can also capture aerial shots of panoramic grandeur once available only to big-budget movie studios. A GoPro Hero 4 cost about $500 in 2016, while drones used in filmmaking started at about $1,000. These prices compare quite favorably to helicopters, which used to be the only way to capture eye-in-the-sky footage. A typical helicopter with a professional film crew costs about $25,000 a day. In contrast, a drone handled by a trained pilot, professional camera operator, and a spotter costs about $5,000.

Drone Film Festival

Economics aside, the future of drones in filmmaking lies in the way the camera-equipped rigs can be put to use creatively. In 2015 the first-ever New York City Drone Film Festival offered a glimpse into that future. Film director Randy Scott Slavin founded the film festival after buying a first-generation DJI Phantom 1 drone in 2014. The Phantom 1 was equipped with a GoPro mount, which added to the quadcopter's popularity. Slavin attracted attention after producing a video called *Aerial NYC*, which showed footage shot from the Phantom as it flew around Manhattan skyscrapers, above taxi-clogged city streets, alongside bridges, and through the famous Washington Square Arch. Slavin could not find any place to air his drone movie, so he founded the Drone Film Festival, which received widespread coverage from major newspapers and online. According to Slavin, "Drones just happened to be scorching hot."[37]

Manhattan skyscrapers (pictured) featured prominently in one of the films shown at the New York City Drone Film Festival. Using a DJI Phantom I drone and GoPro camera, the filmmaker obtained unusual views of Manhattan from the air.

Drone films were so popular that Slavin was able to put together a three-hour show with thirty-five short movies shot by drone. Many of the entries were artistic. They featured scenes from cameras shooting high in the sky to offer soaring overhead scenes of forests, mountains, and other picturesque vistas. The film that attracted the most attention at the festival was the music video "I Won't Let You Down" by the alternative pop band OK Go. The video featured hundreds of choreographed dancers shot from a drone hovering high above.

Some of the other festival entries demonstrated exciting new ways drones were being used to document current events. One of the most dramatic nature films was shot by videographer Eric Cheng. In September 2014 Cheng flew a DJI Phantom 2 drone over the Bardarbunga volcano in Iceland. The rig's GoPro Hero 3 camera captured remarkable footage of red-hot, molten lava bubbling inside the crater and erupting skyward in a wall of fire. Temperatures above the volcano hovered at 2,100°F (1,149°C). Despite donning a gas mask, heavy boots, and protective clothing, Cheng was able to walk only to within a mile of the crater. However, the drone's Wi-Fi was able to transmit video back to Cheng's laptop. Once the drone was retrieved, Cheng saw that the front of the GoPro had melted into bubbled plastic—but only after capturing a close-up glimpse into volcanic fury at its most dramatic. As Cheng commented: "The fact that you can take a $1,000 flying camera and put it in the middle of an erupting volcano to capture wide-angle views of this giant bowl of molten lava, which is exploding and throwing lava 150 meters or so into the air, is pretty amazing."[38]

Drone Journalism

While filmmakers like Cheng document events in the natural world, others are using drones to gather newsworthy images in war zones deemed too dangerous for reporters. One of the most powerful videos demonstrating the possibilities of using a drone for news gathering was produced by Russian camera operator Alexander Pushin. In October 2015 Pushin created *Chronicles of the Drone*, shot in and above the devastated suburb of Jobar in Damascus, Syria. The compelling aerial footage shows Russian tanks maneuvering on the ground as they exchange fire with Syrian rebels. The drone flies through the smoke rising from burning buildings and circles around destroyed apartment complexes. In some scenes Pushin runs tank footage backward and forward, giving the film the appearance of a deadly video game. The power of *Chronicles of the Drone* proved to be too much for some. After receiving numerous complaints about the video, YouTube removed it from its website.

The use of drones for recording current events is not limited to independent filmmakers; most major news organizations are experimenting with what is being called drone journalism. In 2015 at least ten media companies—including the *New York Times*, the Associated Press, the *Washington Post*, and Getty Images—asked the FAA for permission to use drones for gathering news. The push for using drones is largely financial. Helicopters and trained pilots cost a lot of money. In contrast, drones represent a fraction of the cost and can deliver the same type of footage, including aerial shots of fires, natural disasters, police chases, crime scenes, and traffic jams. This has led local TV news stations in Chicago; San Francisco; Jacksonville, Florida; and elsewhere to turn to drones for shooting news footage in 2015.

Red-hot, molten lava flows from Iceland's Bardarbunga volcano, which erupted in 2014. Dramatic footage of the eruption was captured on film by using a DJI Phantom 2 drone and GoPro Hero 3 camera.

Flexibility and Unfortunate Accidents

Current events and public entertainment intersect at sporting events; the public wants to see live coverage of games, and drones can provide the most intimate, entertaining shots of players as they compete. And while drones at sporting events offer promise, there can be problems. This point was clearly illustrated by the use of drones at two separate ski events held eleven months apart.

In January 2015 the sports network ESPN received FAA permission to use drones to cover the Winter X Games in Aspen, Colorado. ESPN outfitted a Vortex Aerial drone with a Panasonic GH4 camera to send live images to producers on the ground via radio waves. Since FAA rules prevent drones from being flown over crowds, the network could only use the device in areas where spectators were not permitted. Athletes were warned that drones would be buzzing nearby as they competed.

The ESPN drone delivered exciting coverage from behind, overhead, and in front of skiers and other athletes. As ESPN vice president Chris Calcinari explained, "Drones allow us to freely move a camera around and above a subject, at varying heights and varying speeds. This untethered flexibility [gives] our production teams the ability to provide angles that have not been seen previously."[39]

> **WORDS IN CONTEXT**
>
> **untethered**
> Free from a rope or wire that restricts movement.

The new technology provided viewers with entertaining shots of the X Games. But the danger posed by drones was clearly illustrated the following December at the International Ski Federation's (FIS) World Cup event in Italy. The ski federation deployed a remote-controlled drone with a mounted camera to follow Olympic silver medalist Marcel Hirscher as he was speeding down a mountain, winding through the flags and poles on a slalom course. Suddenly, the drone crashed down from the sky inches behind Hirscher, who continued to ski, finishing in second place.

The FIS called the crash of the 50-pound (22.7 kg) drone an unfortunate accident and offered an apology. Hirscher issued a statement after the near miss: "This is horrible. This can never

The Drone Racing League

People love watching races between almost anything that moves, including cars, boats, bicycles, wheelchairs, lawn mowers, toboggans, and even school buses. So it should come as no surprise that some drone racing videos on YouTube are drawing more than 1 million views. And 2016 might one day be remembered as the year that drone racing was established as a competitive sport. Competitors in the New York City–based Drone Racing League are leading the way. The league staged six races in 2016 leading to a final World Championship that crowned the first-ever top global drone pilot.

The contests provide a vision of what the drone racing future might look like. Identical drones are supplied to each competitor. Racers cannot make major changes to the drones but can fine-tune the controls and handling characteristics to their individual preferences. Drones can reach speeds of 80 miles per hour (129 kph). Pilots compete in races that last ninety seconds to two minutes, navigating past checkpoints that record times. League founder and CEO Nicholas Horbaczewski is excited about the future of drones and drone racing. He says, "We are in the infancy of drone technology. Although it's already a multi-billion dollar industry. This is the beginning of raising a generation of drone pilots around the globe. The skills and abilities of pilots will only get better as time moves on. It'll be exciting to watch for sure."

Quoted in Dave Pinter, "Drone Racing Prides Itself on Being the Ultimate Spectator Sport," PSFK, February 9, 2016. www.psfk.com.

happen again. This can be a serious injury." However, Hirscher later saw humor in the accident, stating on his Instagram account that there was "heavy air traffic in Italy."[40]

When it came time to prepare for the January 2016 Winter X Games in Aspen, ESPN decided against using drones to cover the event. The network denied that its decision had anything to do with the accident in Italy but did not offer any particular reason. Professional photographer Nathan Bilow thinks the network might be avoiding drones for technical reasons; cold temperatures and the thin air at high altitudes can affect the way drones operate. He says, "It's a great tool, it totally is. But the manufacturers are still working out the kinks."[41]

With an eye toward working out the kinks and improving drone safety, media giants such as the Associated Press and NBCUniversal began working with the Mid-Atlantic Aviation Partnership of Virginia Tech in 2015. The group runs one of six FAA-approved drone test sites in the United States. Rose Mooney, executive director of the aviation partnership, laid out the goals for the project: "Virginia Tech sees this collaboration as a key to groundbreaking research to use UAS [unmanned aircraft systems] for the news and broadcasting industry on a routine basis. UAS can provide this industry a safe, efficient, timely and affordable way to gather and disseminate information and keep journalists out of harm's way."[42]

Racing to Use Drones

While researchers work to improve drones, the demand for them at sporting events continues. In September 2015 the National Football League (NFL) became the first major sports organization to get an FAA exemption allowing the use of drones. However, the NFL had to comply with the agency's ban against drones being flown over crowds. The league plans to use the machines in closed-set locations, zooming over practice fields and empty stadiums being readied for big games.

Although most drones in entertainment have a place behind the camera, some have ended up on center stage. In March 2016 the first-ever World Drone Prix was held in Dubai, United Arab Emirates. The contest featured thirty-two drones racing around what was billed as the only aerial drone racetrack in the world. Drone racing leagues are also forming in the United States. Supporters say it is the spectator sport of the future.

Whether drone races become as common as NASCAR remains an open question. However, in Hollywood, drone production companies are expanding at a rapid rate as stomach-dropping aerial shots become a blockbuster mainstay. Meanwhile, tech companies are racing to improve safety with the goal of convincing the FAA to loosen drone rules. But as long as the whirling drones can accidentally drop out of the sky or fly into a jet plane, the drones in the entertainment business will remain tightly regulated.

Chapter 5

The Future of Consumer Drones

Many tech analysts believe that the future of drones can be found in a bland Boston office building that houses a company called CyPhy (pronounced "sci-fi"). CyPhy is headed by Helen Greiner, the mechanical engineer and robotics expert who cofounded iRobot in 1990. iRobot created the Roomba vacuuming robot as well as robots used by the US military in Iraq and Afghanistan to locate and detonate roadside bombs.

Greiner, who has worked at the National Aeronautics and Space Administration (NASA) Jet Propulsion Laboratory and the Massachusetts Institute of Technology Artificial Intelligence Laboratory, has been called the "Robot Queen" by *Fortune* magazine. She is currently working on making drones smarter and cheaper. In 2015 CyPhy launched a campaign on the crowdfunding website Kickstarter and raised nearly $1 million to fund a next-generation drone called the LVL 1. The $500 white drone, about the size and shape of a large crab and outfitted with six rotors on outstretched arms, was made available to the public in 2016.

A Drone for the Masses

Greiner calls the LVL 1 "the first drone for everyone."[43] To understand why, it is necessary to look at what has previously been available. Most consumer drones sold before 2015 were made up of only a few components; they had four motorized rotors, a remote control, a flight stability system, and a plastic housing. Tech reviewer Casey Newton explains why this basic equipment caused problems for amateur pilots, who often paid more than $1,000 for these drones: "What goes up must come down—and if it's a drone you're talking about, it often comes down in the most unfortunate ways possible. It bounces off a tree trunk, smashes into a highway tunnel, or careens into the side of a building. It runs out of battery and falls into a body of water. Your four-figure investment is typically only as good as your ability to handle it once it's aloft."[44]

In addition to flight problems, most drones required users to invest in their own cameras and gimbals. (A gimbal is a support system for a camera that keeps it in the same position regardless of the motion of the drone.) These additions could cost as much as the drone. But Greiner wants the drone to function "like . . . the next generation of video cameras."[45] Toward that end, the LVL 1 includes a built-in camera and gimbal.

The LVL 1 also contains advanced technology to keep it in the air. The drone's six-rotor design is much more stable than a typical quadcopter. This makes it possible for the drone to

Helen Greiner, cofounder of iRobot, displays a LVL 1 drone during a 2015 presentation about her newest venture, CyPhy. The company produces a next-generation drone that can be used by just about anyone.

change directions without tilting forward, as four-rotor drones do. The six rotors provide stable video footage and make it easier for first-time pilots to fly the drone as soon as they unpack it from the shipping box.

Additionally, the drone does not require a dedicated controller. Users download the Swipe-to-Fly app to their smartphone. The app provides a live video feed from the drone camera. Operators control the craft by moving a finger across the screen on the phone. The app also allows real-time video footage to be shared on social networking sites like Twitter and Facebook.

Unlike many consumer drones, the LVL 1 software includes geofencing. This is an invisible electronic fence that prevents the drone from straying into areas where it should not be flown. For example, parents can set up a geofence around their backyard to keep their children from flying drones into the neighbor's yard. Geofences are also set up around restricted spaces like airports, stadiums, and government buildings.

The Addition of Smart Features

CyPhy is one of several producers seeking to create drones of the future that are cheaper and easier to fly. Manufacturers are also working to incorporate more computing power and better sensors that will give drones the ability to identify objects, respond to voice commands, and use artificial intelligence to avoid crashing. According to Chris Anderson, CEO of 3D Robotics, future drones "need to be smart yet simple."[46]

Some smart features coming to consumer drones are those that can already be found on machines used by the military. Auto-follow, which provides drone surveillance for soldiers on the ground, is one example. This feature enables drones to follow pilots who wear controllers called trackers. The drone homes in on and moves in designated flight paths around the tracker.

A small start-up called Lily Robotics is using auto-follow technology to allow its drone to function as a smart video camera.

Drones Talking to Each Other

Some drones are equipped with geofencing, which stops them from taking off and flying near well-known restricted areas like airports, military bases, and government buildings. However, geofencing is of limited use. The FAA often creates temporary no-go zones around live sporting events, political rallies, and presidential motorcades, and most geofencing software cannot be updated to include these temporary restrictions.

In 2016 software makers were working to create smarter drones with geofencing software that could be constantly updated, in much the same way smartphone maps update traffic conditions. Manufacturers envision drones communicating with an air traffic controller system at a local airport—and with other drones in the sky. To achieve this goal, researchers are working with NASA to build an unmanned traffic management system for drones. The system will rely on geofencing software, satellites, and powerful computers that can track hundreds of small objects flying at low altitudes. This system will allow thousands of consumer drones, package delivery drones, and even passenger drones to operate safely in the same area. As tech writer Tim Moynihan explains, "You can rest assured that toy drones, [expensive] drones, and commercial drones will all be much smarter in the near future. The bigger hurdle is making sure they talk to each other."

Tim Moynihan, "Things Will Get Messy If We Don't Start Wrangling Drones Now," *Wired*, January 30, 2016. www.wired.com.

The Lily drone can be thrown into the air, where it takes off and hovers, awaiting instructions from the watch-like tracker worn on the user's wrist. With one tap of the tracker, the drone can execute a series of complex preprogrammed aerial maneuvers while the camera stays focused on the user. This provides amazing "dronies," or drone selfies.

The Lily can follow a user at speeds of up to 25 miles per hour (40 kph). In the hover-and-aim mode, the drone maintains its position in one location—above a skate ramp or ski jump for example—while tracking the moving user with its camera. In the circle mode, the drone will shoot video footage as it flies around the user.

While the Lily is about as big as a dinner plate, the company's engineers hope to shrink it down to the size of a smartphone.

They envision a future where people pull the Lily from their pockets, toss it in the air, and get great photos that a selfie stick could never provide.

A Fast Flier

In 2010 the French tech company Parrot helped popularize drones when it introduced its AR.Drone. This was one of the first drones produced for the consumer market. In 2016 Parrot was at the forefront once again when it introduced the Disco, a fast, smart drone that weighs only about 1.5 pounds (700 g). By comparison, the popular DJI Phantom 3 weighs about 2.8 pounds (1,280 grams).

The Disco does not rely on helicopter rotors; it is powered by a rear propeller. The fixed-wing drone with a 3.2-foot (1 m) wingspan resembles a mini fighter jet. When not in use, the wings can be removed to make the drone more compact. Because of its aerodynamic shape, which cuts through the air, the Disco can fly up to 50 miles per hour (80 kph), making it faster than most consumer drones, which top out at around 35 miles per hour (56 kph). The shape also makes the drone twice as energy efficient as a quadcopter, allowing the Disco to stay in the air for up to forty-five minutes. Users launch the Disco in the air simply by throwing it. Once in the air, the drone circles autonomously until the user provides instructions. The drone can be flown freestyle or programmed to fly on a preset course.

> **WORDS IN CONTEXT**
>
> **geofencing**
> The use of GPS technology to create a virtual geographic boundary, which grounds or repels a mobile device entering or leaving a particular area.

Seeing and Flying

The Disco's built-in nose camera can take quality photographs and record high-definition video. The Disco camera also works with first person view (FPV) goggles. These goggles mark a new trend in drone technology first introduced in 2014. FPV goggles contain a video receiver that works with a video transmitter on the

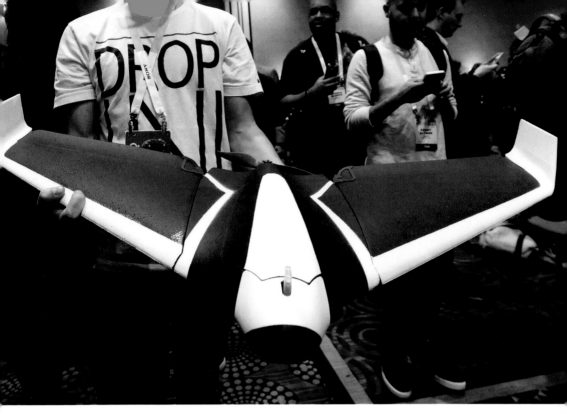

The maker of the fast, smart drone called Disco shows a prototype to members of the media in 2016. The drone's aerodynamic shape helps it fly faster and stay in the air longer than the typical consumer drone.

drone. The view from the camera is transmitted to the goggles; pilots wearing FPV goggles experience the feeling of flying while seeing a drone's-eye-view of the world. As drone reviewer Fintan Corrigan writes, "Flying using the best FPV goggles is a terrific experience. It's a thrilling adventure as you sweep along as if you were the actual drone."[47]

Researchers are working to combine FPV goggles with another hot tech trend, virtual reality (VR). With virtual reality, a person is completely immersed in a computer-generated 3D environment. The VR effect is created by lenses inside a headset that focus the picture separately for each eye. This creates a 3D stereoscopic image that mimics how each eye views the world from a slightly different perspective. The visuals are enhanced by a feat called head tracking. That means when the user's head moves, the picture shifts up and down, side to side, or at an angle, depending on the movements.

Virtual reality headsets like the Oculus Rift and Samsung Gear VR were first made available to consumers in March 2016. The headsets were initially designed for playing video games and watching movies, but retailers and others are coming up with different uses. Some of the Lowe's home improvement stores, for instance, have installed a space that enables shoppers to see a 3D virtual reality mock-up of their renovation plans.

Virtual reality and head-tracking technology are also being applied to drones. The prototype FLYBi drone, created in 2015 by Tim Voss in Santa Clara, California, comes with a headset that streams live high-definition video from the drone while it is flying. A built-in sensor in the headset allows pilots to direct the drone by turning their heads in whatever direction they want the machine to fly.

VR Videos Shot with a Drone

While VR headsets are being used to guide drones, GoPro is developing a camera that will allow drones to shoot VR videos. The videos will provide a full 360-degree view of a drone flight to someone wearing a VR headset. To make this concept reality, GoPro unveiled a prototype VR six-camera spherical array in 2015. The six cameras shoot 360 degrees of video, which is pulled together into one VR film by the array's software.

While GoPros have long been attached to the underbellies of drones, the Six-Camera Spherical Array was designed to work with a GoPro-built drone called the Karma, which the company hoped to sell to consumers by 2017. Pilots flying the Karma while wearing VR headsets should be able to view the world as birds, flying above the landscape while looking around in any direction.

Keeping Drones in the Air

One of the downsides to shooting video with drone-mounted cameras is that the videos have to be short. The typical drone

Out-of-Control Drones

In January 2015 a DJI Phantom flown by an amateur pilot in Washington, DC, crashed on the White House lawn at three o'clock in the morning. While President Obama was not there at the time, the quadcopter triggered a Secret Service lockdown. The pilot later said he lost control of the drone earlier in the day, several blocks away; he had no intention of flying it near the White House.

The White House drone crash was one of hundreds of incidents in 2015 related to amateur pilots either ignoring or ignorant of FAA rules concerning places drones may operate. For example, drones are prohibited from flying anywhere in or around Washington, DC. Despite the restrictions, the Pentagon (which is the biggest user of drones in the world) was forced to put up a sign that says "No Drone Zone" to keep amateur fliers from buzzing its grounds.

The FAA also bans drones from flying within 5 miles (8 km) of airports and above 400 feet (122 m). Despite those rules, from August 2015 to January 2016 there were 583 drone sightings at American airports. In Los Angeles a drone was spotted by a jet pilot at 5,700 feet (1,737 m). In Riverside, California, a pilot saw a drone at 9,000 feet (2,743). Most drones weigh less than the 55-pound (25 kg) maximum permitted by the FAA. But a stray drone of any size could easily bring down a jet that is flying hundreds of miles per hour.

can be in the air for only twenty-five minutes before its batteries need to be recharged for up to two hours. And keeping drones in the air for longer periods has been one of the major challenges facing manufacturers. The batteries in drones are heavy, so making them bigger only adds more weight—and more weight means shorter flight times. But a Massachusetts company called Top Flight is tackling the problem, tapping the same type of technology used in hybrid automobiles like the Chevy Volt.

The Top Flight drone has a small, efficient gasoline-powered motor, which runs a generator that charges the drone's batteries. This gives the drone a two-hour flight time even while carrying a payload such as a camera. As Top Flight CEO John Polo explains: "The hybrid engine is an onboard generator. It's generating juice all the time. It's generating juice for the motors, and it's generating juice for the electronics and whatever is on the payload."[48]

An English power-technology company is using another type of automobile technology to keep drones in the air longer. In 2016 Intelligent Energy built a drone powered by a hydrogen fuel cell. In cars, hydrogen fuel cells combine hydrogen and oxygen to produce electricity, which in turn runs the motor. The lightweight fuel cell created by Intelligent Energy works the same way, allowing a drone to stay in the air for as long as two hours. There is one drawback, however. A small hydrogen fuel cell costs around $1,000, while typical drone batteries cost less than $100.

Flying a Passenger Drone

Whatever their power source, most consumer drones are used to shoot bird's-eye-view photos and videos. But the Chinese inventor Huazhi Hu thinks drones should do more than that. Hu's company, Ehang, has developed an eight-rotor octocopter drone, or autonomous aerial vehicle (AAV). The drone, called the Ehang 184, is meant to be used as a personal transportation device. Hu originally designed the drone after a small plane crash killed two of his friends. The Ehang 184 was meant to be used during flight emergencies; instead of using a parachute, a pilot in distress could glide safely to earth in a single-seat drone. After working with the drone, Hu realized the Ehang 184 could also be used to transport a single individual.

The Ehang 184, which made its first appearance at the 2016 Consumer Electronics Show in Las Vegas, Nevada, requires little input from passengers. Travelers climb in, select their destination on a touch screen tablet display, and press the takeoff button. The drone has an automated flight system that takes over, guiding the craft to its destination along the fastest route. The AAV relies on obstacle-avoidance features and a communications system that automatically contacts other aircraft and air traffic controllers at airports to ensure a safe landing. The drone can also stop and hover in place if necessary.

The Ehang 184 is capable of carrying up to 264 pounds (120 kg), has a maximum speed of 62 miles per hour (100 kph), and can reach a maximum altitude of 11,480 feet (3,499 m). However, the AAV has a flight time of only twenty-three minutes before its

Inventor Huazhi Hu's company has developed an eight-propeller octocopter drone for use as a personal transportation device. The Ehang 184 (pictured in 2016) has an automated flight system that guides the craft along the fastest route until it reaches its destination.

power runs out. While Hu hopes to sell the Ehang 184 for around $250,000, few expect to see the drone in American skies; it is unlikely the FAA will approve AAVs anytime soon.

Drones, Regulations, and the Future

The FAA, originally created to regulate private and commercial airplanes, will likely be grappling with many drone issues in the future. Dramatic improvements in drone technology and rapid price decreases have helped fuel a consumer market for drones. As drone ownership becomes more widespread, regulation will likely also increase. Safety is probably the biggest concern, as noted by California senator Dianne Feinstein in 2015: "It's clear that reckless consumer drone use is increasing."[49] Reports of potentially dangerous incidents are rising. Consumer drones are being flown in restricted airspace around airports, military bases, and government buildings, including the White House and the Pentagon in Washington, DC. While the military uses radar to monitor aircraft in Washington, drones fly low and slow, making them invisible to radar.

Amateur drone pilots have also been interfering with firefighting aircraft that dump water, foams, and gels on fires. In 2015 the US Forest Service had to divert aircraft away from fast-moving fires twenty-five times due to drones in the vicinity. The city of Poway, California, dealt with the issue by passing an ordinance banning drones from flying within 2 miles (3.2 km) of wildfires or other public emergencies. Poway is also home to General Atomics Aeronautical Systems, builders of the Reaper and Predator UAVs that are used by the military. As Poway's mayor Steve Vaus points out, "There's a great irony that one of the world's largest drone manufacturers is based here . . . [but we wanted] to protect our fire responders."[50]

Wherever drones are flown, there are also concerns over privacy. In recent years numerous incidents have been reported where people have seen drones hovering over their backyards or outside their windows. One well-publicized incident involved William Merideth, a Kentucky man who saw a drone fly by his property three times within a half hour. Merideth pulled out a shotgun and blasted the drone out of the sky. Merideth was charged with felony endangerment, but his case was dismissed by a sympathetic judge.

The stories of drone dangers, which appear in the media almost daily, have done little to slow the popularity of the tiny aircraft. While the FAA struggles to regulate drones, bigger, better, smarter, and longer-flying machines are being brought to market every day. While drone enthusiasts dream of flying to work in their AAVs, regulators continue to mull ways to strictly manage and control the use of drones. So even as drone sales soar, the future for consumer drones remains up in the air.

Source Notes

Introduction: Incredibly Versatile Machines

1. Kit Eaton, "Civilian Photography, Now Rising to New Level," *New York Times*, January 1, 2014. www.nytimes.com.
2. Eaton, "Civilian Photography, Now Rising to New Level."
3. Quoted in Matt Alderton, "To the Rescue! Why Drones in Police Work Are the Future of Crime Fighting," Line/Shape/Space, April 30, 2015. http://lineshapespace.com.
4. Craig Whitlock, "FAA Records Detail Hundreds of Close Calls Between Airplanes and Drones," *Washington Post*, August 20, 2015. www.washingtonpost.com.

Chapter 1: Drones of War

5. Quoted in Phil Stewart, "U.S. Strikes al Shabaab Training Camp in Somalia, More than 150 Killed," Reuters, March 8, 2016. www.reuters.com.
6. Annie Jacobsen, *The Pentagon's Brain*. New York: Little, Brown, 2015, p. 452.
7. Quoted in Adrian Shaw, "The Eight Inch Spy in the Sky: Tiny 'Black Hornet' Helicopters Snoop in Afghanistan," *Mirror* (London), February 3, 2013. www.mirror.co.uk.
8. Quoted in Shaw, "The Eight Inch Spy in the Sky."
9. Quoted in Jacobsen, *The Pentagon's Brain*, p. 474.
10. Quoted in Jeff Goodell, "The Rise of Intelligent Machines, Part 1," *Rolling Stone*, March 10, 2016, p. 48.
11. Ray Mabus, "SECNAV's Prepared Remarks at Sea-Air-Space 2015," Navy Live, April 15, 2015. http://navylive.dodlive.mil.
12. David Hambling, *Swarm Troopers: How Small Drones Will Conquer the World*. Seattle: Amazon Digital Services, 2015, p. 21.
13. Quoted in Kevin McCaney, "Day of the LOCUST: Navy Demonstrates Swarming UAVs," Defense Systems, April 15, 2015. https://defensesystems.com.
14. Hambling, *Swarm Troopers*, pp. 416–17.

15. Quoted in Allen McDuffee, "U.S. Navy Gets In on Drone Action with First Real Aircraft Carrier Landing," *Wired*, July 25, 2013. www.wired.com.
16. Quoted in Goodell, "The Rise of Intelligent Machines, Part 1," p. 48.
17. Pedro Domingos, *The Master Algorithm*. New York: Basic Books, p. 281.

Chapter 2: Law Enforcement Eyes in the Sky

18. Quoted in Peter Holley, "The Latest Policing Tool to Monitor Rowdy Spring Breakers: Drones," *Washington Post*, March 9, 2016. www.washingtonpost.com.
19. Quoted in Kristen E. Boon and Douglas C. Lovelace, eds., *The Domestic Use of Unmanned Aerial Vehicles*. New York: Oxford University Press, 2014, p. 4.
20. Sean Varah, "5 Ways Drones Can Help Cops Fight Crime," PoliceOne, September 17, 2015. www.policeone.com.
21. Quoted in David Larkins, "Drones Give RCMP 'New Perspective' of Crime Scenes," *Winnipeg Sun*, August 30, 2014. www.winnipegsun.com.
22. Quoted in David Casillas, "Scientists Create Drones Used to Find Lost Hikers," *Metro*, February 25, 2016. www.metro.us.
23. Quoted in Casillas, "Scientists Create Drones Used to Find Lost Hikers."
24. Thomas Snitch, "Drones Help Rangers Fight Poachers," *Wild Things* (blog), *Slate*, January 28, 2015. www.slate.com.
25. Quoted in Carol Cratty, "FBI Uses Drones for Surveillance in the U.S.," CNN, June 20, 2013. www.cnn.com.
26. Michael Peck, "Predator Drone Sends North Dakota Man to Jail," *Forbes*, January 27, 2014. www.forbes.com.
27. Quoted in *New York Post*, "FBI Behind Mysterious Surveillance Aircraft over US Cities," June 2, 2015. http://nypost.com.

Chapter 3: The Business of Drones

28. Quoted in John Biggs, "The FAA Shuts Down Beer-Delivery Drone," TechCrunch, February 4, 2014. http://techcrunch.com.

29. Quoted in James Quinn, "Amazon's Jeff Bezos: With Jeremy Clarkson We're Entering a New Golden Age of Television," *Telegraph* (London), August 6, 2015. www.telegraph.co.uk.

30. Quoted in Jennifer Hall, "CEA Signs On as First Major Supporter of UAS Safety Campaign, 'Know Before You Fly,'" Know Before You Fly, January 7, 2015. http://knowbeforeyou fly.org.

31. Quoted in Christopher Doering, "Growing Use of Drones Poised to Transform Agriculture," *USA Today*, March 23, 2014. www.usatoday.com.

32. Quoted in Mary Esch, "Utilities See Potential in Drones to Inspect Power Lines, Towers," *Los Angeles Daily News*, November 22, 2015. www.dailynews.com.

33. Quoted in Wendy Koch, "Drones Soar as Energy's Inspector Gadget at Pipelines, Windmills," National Geographic, September 23, 2015. http://news.nationalgeographic.com.

34. Mark Zuckerberg, "Is Connectivity a Human Right?," Facebook, August 2013, www.facebook.com/isconnectivityahum anright.

35. Mark Zuckerberg, "Connecting the World from the Sky," Facebook, 2014. http://newsroom.fb.com.

Chapter 4: Entertainment, News, and Sports

36. Quoted in *Rotor Drone Magazine*, "Drones on Set: Shooting *The Expendables 3*," January 12, 2015. www.rotordrone mag.com.

37. Quoted in Greg Cook, "Drones Are Changing How We See— and Think About—Our World," ARTery, September 14, 2015. http://artery.wbur.org.

38. Quoted in Rheana Murray, "Drone Captures Incredible Footage of Volcano Eruption," ABC News, October 2, 2014. http://abcnews.go.com.

39. Quoted in Edgar Alvarez, "ESPN Is Bringing Camera Drones to the X Games," Engadget, January 21, 2015. www.engad get.com.

40. Quoted in Matias Grez, "Drone Crashes onto Piste, Misses Champion Skier by Inches," CNN, December 23, 2015. http://edition.cnn.com.

41. Quoted in Madeleine Osberger, "X Games Drone Use Shot Down," *Aspen (CO) Daily News Online*, January 4, 2016. www.aspendailynews.com.

42. Quoted in Charles D. Tobin, "News Media Coalition Announces Partnership to Test Small News Drones at FAA Test Site," Holland & Knight, January 15, 2015. www.hklaw.com.

Chapter 5: The Future of Consumer Drones

43. Quoted in Andrew Moseman, "Is CyPhy's LV 1 Really the 'Drone for Everybody?,'" *Popular Mechanics*, May 13, 2015. www.popularmechanics.com.

44. Casey Newton, "The 3D Robotics Solo May Be the Smartest Drone Ever," Verge, April 13, 2015. www.theverge.com.

45. Quoted in Patricia Sellers, "Robot Queen Takes to the Skies," *Fortune*, July 13, 2015. http://fortune.com.

46. Quoted in James Trew, "3D Robotics: The Future of Drones Needs to Be Smart Yet Simple," Engadget, January 6, 2016. www.engadget.com.

47. Fintan Corrigan, "FPV Goggles for Drones and Experiencing the Thrill of Flying," DroneZon, March 25, 2016. www.dronezon.com.

48. Quoted in Michael Belfiore, "Hybrid Power Could Let Drones Fly for Hours," *Popular Mechanics*, April 3, 2015. www.popularmechanics.com.

49. Quoted in Lucy Shouten, "Drones out of Control: What Is Congress Doing?," *Christian Science Monitor*, October 1, 2015. www.csmonitor.com.

50. Quoted in W.J. Hennigan and Brian Bennett, "Officials Taking Aim at Drone Use," *Los Angeles Times*, April 1, 2016. www.latimes.com.

For Further Research

Books

John Baichtal, *Building Your Own Drones.* Indianapolis: Que, 2016.

Racquel Foran, *Robotics.* Minneapolis: Essential Library, 2015.

Greenhaven Press, ed., *Drones.* Farmington Hills, MI; Cengage, 2016.

Stuart Kallen, *Cutting Edge Entertainment.* San Diego, CA: ReferencePoint, 2017.

Mark Lafay, *Drones for Dummies.* Hoboken, NJ: Wiley, 2015.

Don Nardo, *How Robotics Is Changing Society.* San Diego, CA: ReferencePoint, 2016.

Websites

Aerial MOB (http://aerialmob.com). This Southern California filmmaking company was the first in the nation to receive official FAA permission to shoot television and movie scenes using drones. The company's website features numerous eye-catching clips shot with drones, including commercials used in the 2016 Super Bowl telecast.

Bureau of Investigative Journalism: Covert Drone War (www.thebureauinvestigates.com/category/projects/drones). The London-based Bureau of Investigative Journalism has been tracking the wars waged by the United States and its allies in Afghanistan, Iraq, Yemen, and Somalia since 2001. The Covert Drone War page provides accurate information on the number of strikes, civilians killed, and other details.

DIY Drones (www.diydrones.com). The *DIY Drones* blog contains more than eleven thousand articles on the latest news, updates, and changes in the massive do-it-yourself drone community. Visitors can learn how to build or improve their own equipment and can find information on dozens of drone-related topics.

DroneLife (http://dronelife.com). DroneLife offers buying guides, news updates, FAA regulations, and other comprehensive information concerning drones for consumers, businesses, agricultural interests, and security personnel.

Dronethusiast (www.dronethusiast.com). This site was founded by two self-described drone maniacs named Nic and Zsolt, who together provide tips, tutorials, news, and reviews about drones.

My First Drone (http://myfirstdrone.com). Hosted by Korey Smith, this is one of the most popular drone sites, with buying guides, reviews, want ads, and articles about building and flying drones.

New York City Drone Film Festival (www.nycdronefilmfestival .com). The website of the first-ever drone film festival features video clips from Dronie winners of various categories, including Best Extreme Sports, Best Technical, and Best News & Documentary.

Swarm Troopers (www.swarm-troopers.com). This website is hosted by tech journalist David Hambling, who wrote a book of the same name. Hambling blogs about tiny lethal drones like the Raven and Switchblade and provides images and scenarios based on the concept of drone swarms going to war.

VideoUniversity (www.videouniversity.com). VideoUniversity is heavily focused on aerial videography, and the site offers to help people with the art, technology, and business of making drone videos.

Video

Rise of the Drones. DVD. Directed by Peter Yost. Boston: Pangloss Films, 2013.

Index

Picture Credits

About the Author

Stuart A. Kallen is the author of more than 350 nonfiction books for children and young adults. He has written on topics ranging from the theory of relativity to the art of electronic dance music. In addition, Kallen has written award-winning children's videos and television scripts. In his spare time he is a singer, songwriter, and guitarist in San Diego.